Starting a Band

Kathy Galashan

Published in association with The Basic Skills Agency

Hodder & Stoughton

A MEMBER OF THE HODDER HEADLINE GROUP

Acknowledgements
Cover: © Mark Allan/Alpha

Photos: p4 All Action; p8 Mark Allan/Alpha; p12 Neil Munns/'PA' Photos; p15 Suzi Gibbons/Referns; p19 Suzi Gibbons/Redferns; p23 Ashley Knotek/Alpha; p26 Jonathan Furniss

Every effort has been made to trace copyright holders of material reproduced in this book. Any rights not acknowledged will be acknowledged in subsequent printings if notice is given to the publisher.

Orders; please contact Bookpoint Ltd, 39 Milton Park, Abingdon, Oxon OX14 4TD. Telephone (44) 01235 400414, Fax: (44) 01235 400454. Lines are open from 9.00–6.00, Monday to Saturday, with a 24-hour message answering service. Email address: orders@bookpoint.co.uk

British Library Cataloguing in Publication Data
A catalogue record for this title is available from the British Library

ISBN 0 340 80075 5

First published 2001
Impression number   10 9 8 7 6 5 4 3 2 1
Year   2007 2006 2005 2004 2003 2002 2001

Typeset by SX Composing DTP, Rayleigh, Essex
Printed in Great Britain for Hodder & Stoughton Educational, a division of Hodder Headline Plc, 338 Euston Road, London NW1 3BH by Redwood Books, Trowbridge, Wiltshire

Contents

I'm John.
I love music.
I love live music.
I go to gigs
in clubs and pubs.
In the summer I go to music festivals

I watch music videos
and MTV on satellite TV.

I play drums.
I started when I was about ten.
I got a drum kit for Christmas
and practised at home.
I couldn't use the full kit
because it was too noisy.
So I used practise pads.

I've never had lessons
but friends help me.
I watch and listen to other drummers.
Then I try to copy them.
I want to be in a band.
I want to find out
how to get started.

I'm Ben.
I'm in a rock band.
I play bass guitar.
I've made albums
and been on tour.
I play festivals
and support big bands.
The band hasn't hit the big time
but we've been on *Top of the Pops*
and have done OK.

1 First Things First

John   What do you like best
about being in a band?

Ben   That's easy.
I play music.
I love playing with other people.
I love playing to an audience.
Nothing beats a live gig
when the audience is with you.
I feel great
when people are stamping,
cheering and whistling.
There are shouts of 'More, more, more'.
Doing an encore is the best.

Every day is different.
You never know what is coming.
A gig can be great or awful.
It depends on the place, the band
and the audience.

It took Travis six years before they became famous.

John   What about money?
Are you rich?

Ben   Some bands get really rich.
Pop stars are some of the richest people
in the world.
But it takes talent and luck.
Many groups spend years playing
before they get famous.
Travis played for six years.
Everyone said they were rubbish.
Then they hit the big time.
Six years is a long time
when nothing is going your way.

You have to love music.
Start a band
if you want to play.
If you're in it for the money
you'll give up.
You'll never make it.

When you start
it costs you money.
Sometimes you get paid for a gig,
sometimes you don't.
You can pay for rehearsing,
for demo tapes
and for equipment.

Getting started is hard.
But there is always the chance
of the big time.

2 Getting Started

John   How do I get started?

Ben   You have an instrument
and you are practising.
That's a start.
You need to work out
what sort of band
you want to be in.
Then you need
people to play with.

There are two main ways
of getting a band together.
You can form a band with friends
or you can join a band
that already exists.

With a lot of hard work you could appear on *Top of the Pops*.
Just like Tom Jones and the Stereophonics.

Bands advertise for players.
Look in music magazines like *NME*.
Bands will ask you to audition.
They will ask you
to play some songs with them.
If they like you
and you like them
you're in.

John   Sometimes I practise with two friends.
One plays keyboard and
the other plays bass.
The keyboard player sings.

Ben   You can put in an advert
to find another guitarist.
Or just ask around.
Our band started like that.
There were three of us.
Then a friend of a friend
heard about us.
Suddenly we were a band.

3 Rehearsing

Ben   It's good to practise
with other people.
That's when you
begin to develop a style.
The band swaps ideas
and tries out new things.
That's also when rows happen.
Different people have different ideas
about what sounds good.

You need a place to practise.
We practised in a bedroom.
We couldn't use amps, but
we still worked out
how we wanted to sound.
We worked out
what we wanted to play.

I've practised at college,
in a garage,
in a room over a pub –
all sorts of places.

You can also rent
local rehearsal studios.
You get space,
a small p.a. and microphones.
Rehearsal studios can cost
between £5 and £15 an hour.
It's cheaper outside big cities.
Some studios let you record
for a few pounds.
It's not good quality
but you can hear
what you sound like.

Using the rehearsal studios can be expensive
and time consuming.

4 Gigs

John   How did we find places to play?

Ben   Parties are a good way to begin.
You can play at friends' parties
or have your own.
Get together with another band
and put on a local gig.

Schools and colleges are good places.
You may not be paid.
In fact it may cost you money –
but it's a start.
Talk your way into gigs.
Talk to anyone and everyone.
Tell them you're the best.

Don't forget
the band will need equipment.
You will need a p.a.,
microphones and speakers.
You can hire equipment
or buy your own.
In our band each person
brings what they need.
The drummer just brings the drum kit.
You'll also need transport
for your equipment.

It's a good idea
to do a recording.
Send it away.
Let people listen to you.
Then they may give you a gig.

To start a band you need the right equipment, like amps,
microphones and instruments.

5 Recordings

John   So how do we do a recording?
Is it very difficult?
How long should it be?
And what about money?

Ben   First decide on your songs.
Three songs are good.
Maybe write one song yourselves
and do two covers.
A cover is when
you record an old song.
Good songs have been recorded
by lots of groups.
Think of 'My Way'.
That has been covered
by punk, rock and pop bands,
and of course Frank Sinatra.

Practise as a band.
Studio time is too expensive
for rehearsals.

When it's sounding good
you can hire
a recording studio for the day.
A day costs from £150
to £10,000 or more.
Three songs may take
ten hours or so.
A studio has
all the equipment you need.

Set up the equipment.
A studio tape may have
eight tracks or more.
Some studios have 64 tracks.

We record the drums first.
Then we record bass and guitars.
Vocals are recorded next
and then backing vocals.
Each goes on a separate track.

We record each song
a few times.
Then we pick the best bits.

The tracks are put together, or mixed.
Some bits are distorted.
Others made louder.
Tracks are mixed for stereo effect.
Some sounds come
out of the left channel.
Some come out of the right.

Recording studios can use mixing desks to create different sound effects.

In some studios
you do the mixing yourself.
Often there is a person
who does that job for you.

The finished tracks are put
on to a master tape.
Then you can make records,
CDs or cassettes.

I think CDs are best.
The studio may help
to put the master tape on to CD.
Or you can go to a company.
To make 50 CDs
will cost you about £200.

John   Is that the only way
to get a recording?
Can I do it myself?

Ben   Yes you can.
You will need a 4-track
or 8-track tape recorder
and microphones.

Another way is to use a computer.
You can buy a live sound card
which lets you put live music
into your computer.
You can use the computer
to remix the sounds
and put tracks onto a CD.
The quality can be very good.

It is good to do it yourself.
You learn a lot
and you have control
over the sound.

Doing a music or media course
at college helps.
Then you get an idea of equipment
and learn the skills.

6 Fame

John   How do I become famous?
I want people
to recognise me in the street.
I want people to want me.
I'd love to go on tour.

Ben   A band is not all glamour.
Tours are hard work.
We drive around in a bus for days.
It's travelling and playing.
You get to see a lot of places.
We've played France, Sweden, all over.

Often it's great.
A good gig is fantastic.
It's easy to make friends.
Everyone wants to know you.
You have music to talk about.
Then it's time to move on.

Sometimes it's crazy.
When everything goes wrong
it can be a real strain.
Partying and playing burn you out.
Some bands turn to drink and drugs.

Performing at live gigs can be hard work but it is
rewarding.

To become famous you need luck.
But you need to work hard too.
You need a recording company
and a manager.

Recording companies look for talent.
Send them CDs
and tell them where you play.
You have to wait.
You have to be spotted.
That's why bands have a gimmick.
They want to stand out.
Image gets you noticed
as much as good music.

If you're lucky
a recording company
will sign you up.
They will offer you a recording deal.
It's not fame –
but it is the first big step.
Companies give money up front
and arrange records and publicity.

7 Managers

John   Why do we need a manager?

Ben   It's good to have a manager.
A good manager sells a band.
He sends out demos. He keeps a diary.
He makes sure
everyone is at the right place
at the right time.
He looks after the money.
He makes deals.
He sees to transport.

Someone has to do all that.
You don't need a manager –
it could be a band member.
Or you could share out the jobs.
But someone has to understand
deals and money.
Someone has to arrange gigs.
Ask other bands.
See if they've got a good manager.

Good luck.
You'll be needing it.
Enjoy playing.
I hope you make it.

Some managers are just as famous as the band they
promote. As Ronan Keating proves with Westlife.

Finding Out More

NME (New Musical Express) is a music paper
full of ads and articles.

To find out about recording studios,
look in Yellow Pages under 'Recording Services –
Sound'.

To find out about Practise rooms
look in Yellow Pages under 'Music Studios and
Practise Rooms'.

Useful Courses
Local colleges run performing arts courses,
music courses and studio sound courses.
Ask at a career's advice centre or your local library.

Contact the Musicians' Union at:
60/62 Clapham Road
London
SW9 0JJ

Glossary of Terms Used

Amp   Equipment that makes the music louder.

Cover   A song that someone else has already recorded.

Demo   A tape of CD you make to show what you can do.

Gig   A show.

PA   The loud speakers or sound system.

Practise pads A kit that lets you practise but doesn't make a noise.

Track   1. Song on a record or CD.
                   2. An 8-track tape has 8 sections running along the length of the tape.
                      A track is one section.

Vocals   Words of a song.